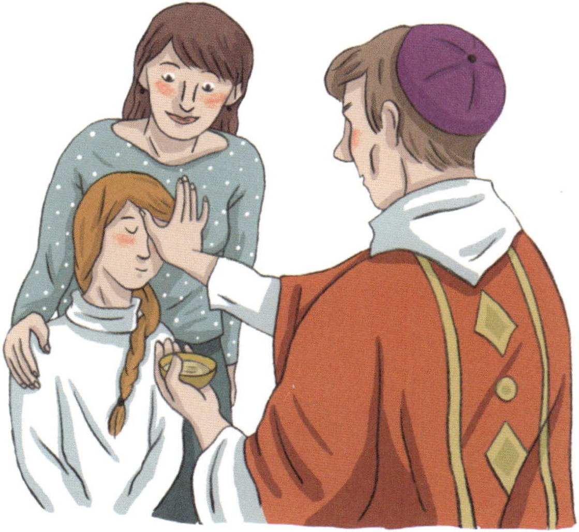

IMPRIMATUR
+ Most Reverend Robert J. McManus, s.t.d.
Bishop of Worcester
January 20, 2020

Scripture texts in this work are taken from the *New American Bible*, revised edition © 2010, 1991, 1986, 1970 Confraternity of Christian Doctrine, Washington, D.C. and are used by permission of the copyright owner. All Rights Reserved. No part of the *New American Bible* may be reproduced in any form without permission in writing from the copyright owner.

© 2020 Pflaum Publishing Group, a division of Bayard, Inc. All rights reserved.
No part of this text may be reproduced in any way or for any use without the written permission of the publisher.

Pflaum Publishing Group
3055 Kettering Blvd., Suite 100
Dayton, OH 45439
800-543-4383
Pflaum.com

ISBN: 978-1-94735-825-6

Printed in China.

bayard   A division of Bayard, Inc.

Text by Anne-Sophie du Bouëtiez • Illustrations by Anne Hemstege

The Sacrament of Confirmation
RECEIVING THE HOLY SPIRIT

Pflaum
SACRAMENTAL PREPARATION

"The wind blows where it wills,
and you can hear the sound it makes,
but you do not know where it comes from
or where it goes; so it is with everyone
who is born of the Spirit."

« JOHN 3:38 »

Contents

WHO IS THE HOLY SPIRIT?............. 8

The Holy Spirit in the Bible.................... 10

The Father, the Son, and the Holy Spirit 14

Pictures and names to talk
about the Holy Spirit......................... 16

WHAT DOES THE HOLY SPIRIT DO? 24

The Seven Gifts of the Holy Spirit 26

Charisms..................................... 28

The Holy Spirit leads us to love
and forgiveness............................... 32

We are "children of God" 34

RECEIVE THE HOLY SPIRIT 36

Baptism: born of the Spirit 38

Confirmation: God renews his gifts 40

In other sacraments 48

The Mass and the Eucharist................... 50

LIVING ACCORDING TO THE HOLY SPIRIT 52

How do you live according to the Spirit? 54

Obstacles to the action of the Spirit 58

Prayers to the Holy Spirit 60

Who is the Holy Spirit?

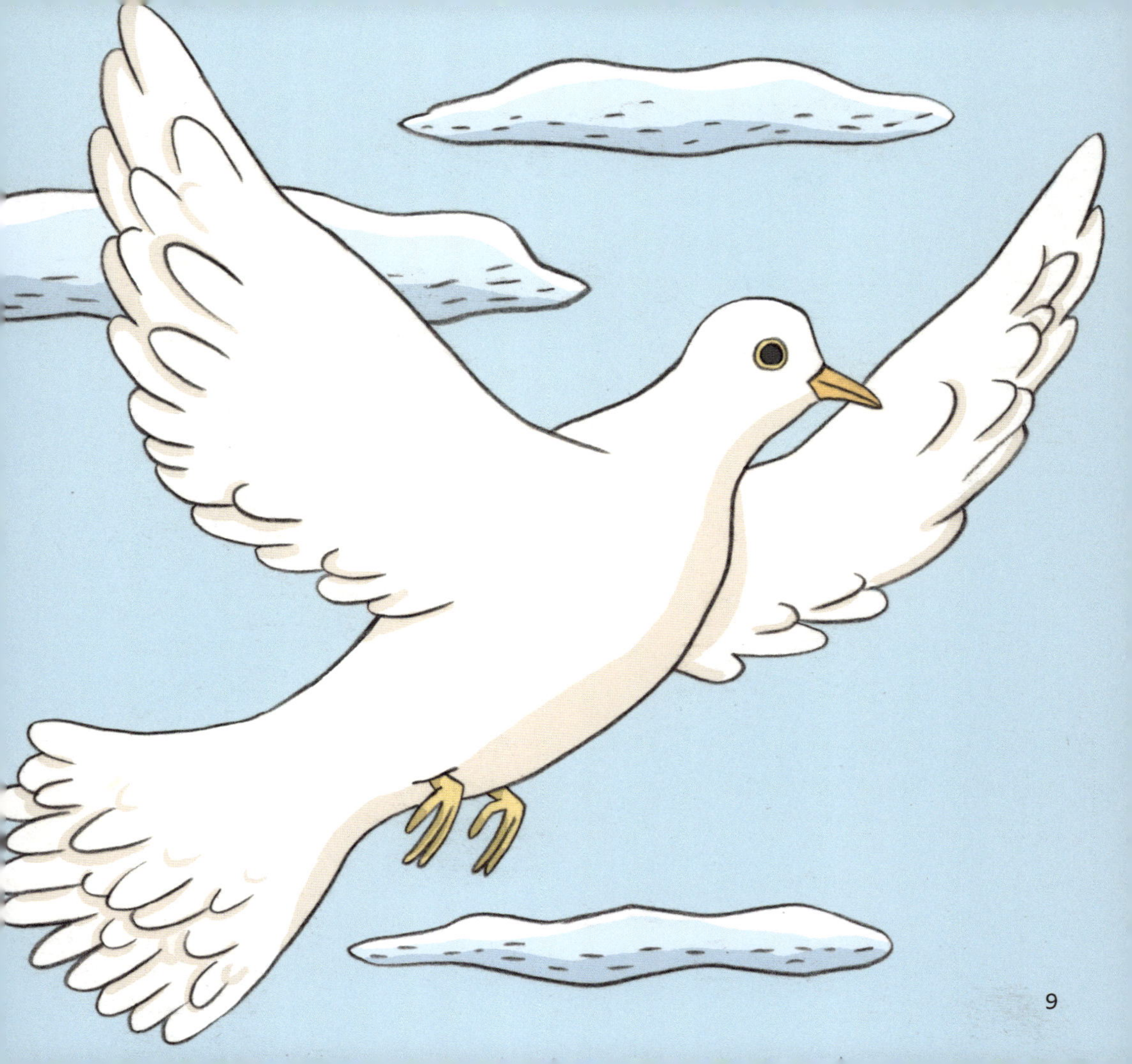

The Holy Spirit in the Bible

The New Testament tells us of the Holy Spirit, the one by whom Jesus was conceived, and who rests in him. After Jesus' Resurrection from the dead, Jesus gave this Spirit to his disciples so that through them, the Word of God would reach the ends of the earth. This Spirit has always been present. In the Old Testament, the People of God recognized the Spirit's action and presence, but they called the Spirit "God's breath"—a force that comes upon a person and gives him or her the courage to speak in the name of God.

WHAT IS A SPIRIT?

We know that every human being has a mysterious source of life inside. We don't completely understand it, but we call this life-source "spirit."

A BREATH THAT CREATES

From the first book of the Bible, from the first sentence, we read about "the breath of God" (in Greek, *pneuma*; in Hebrew, *ruah*). This breath of God is present from the beginning.

"In the beginning, . . . God created the heavens and the earth and the earth was without form or shape, with darkness over the abyss and a mighty wind sweeping over the waters" (Genesis 1:1–2).

It is this breath of God that creates and organizes the world, giving it harmony and order.

A little later in the Bible, Genesis speaks of the creation of man: "Then the Lord . . . blew into his nostrils the breath of life, and the man became a living being" (Genesis 2:7). This is a wonderful image to help us understand that it is God who gives life to everyone.

AN ACTIVE POWER

In the Old Testament, the Spirit comes upon people who are often very humble so that they can accomplish a mission that requires boldness and authority. For example, in the Book of Exodus, God lets Moses know that he is going to fill a man called Bezalel with the presence of God: "See, I have singled out Bezalel. . . . have filled him with a divine spirit of skill and understanding and knowledge" (Exodus 31:2–5).

In the Book of Judges, Gideon is clothed with God's Spirit to free the people (see Judges 6) who are enslaved. Then later, God equips Samson with power to fight the Philistines (see Judges 15).

THE SPIRIT OF GOD GIVEN TO ALL

In the Book of Ezekiel, God chooses to send the Spirit not only to one person but to everyone. God addresses the prophet Ezekiel and asks him to tell the people "I will put my spirit within you so that you walk in my statutes, observe my ordinances, and keep them" (Ezekiel 26:27).

In the Book of Joel, God announces that the Spirit will be spread over all people regardless of race or state of life: "It shall come to pass I will pour out my spirit upon all flesh. Your sons and daughters will prophesy, your old men will dream dreams, your young men will see visions. Even upon your male and female servants, in those days, I will pour out my spirit" (Joel 3:1,2).

JESUS AND THE HOLY SPIRIT

Throughout his life and in his words, Jesus revealed who the Spirit of God is. Although the prophets and kings occasionally refused to follow the Spirit's guidance, Jesus never did. He always spoke by the Spirit and never acted outside the will of the Spirit. John says that the Spirit was with Jesus at all times.

Jesus was conceived by the power of the Holy Spirit. The Spirit overshadowed Mary to enable her to give birth to a son. The angel said to Mary: "The Holy Spirit will come upon you" (Luke 1:35).

The Holy Spirit descended on Jesus during his baptism in the Jordan: "And the Holy Spirit descended upon him in bodily form like a dove" (Luke 3:22).

The same Spirit led Jesus to the desert to fight the three great temptations that tempt every person. These are the temptations to turn to power, to greed, and to self-satisfaction, rather than trusting in God.

"Filled with the Holy Spirit, Jesus returned from the Jordan and was led by the Spirit into the desert for forty days, to be tempted by the devil" (Luke 4:1–2).

Through the power of the Holy Spirit, Jesus was the victor.

Before entering into his Passion and Death, Jesus announced to his disciples that he would not leave them alone. He would send them a defender. "And I will ask the Father, and he will give you another Advocate to be with you always, the Spirit of truth" (John 14:16–17).

THE APOSTLES AND THE HOLY SPIRIT

Fifty days after Easter (also on the Jewish feast of Pentecost), the Apostles received the Holy Spirit. They were empowered to announce that Jesus, who had been crucified, was risen, and was alive again.

Pentecost

"When the time for Pentecost was fulfilled, they were all in one place together. And suddenly there came from the sky a noise like a strong driving wind, and it filled the entire house in which they were. Then there appeared to them tongues as of fire, which parted and came to rest on each one of them. And they were all filled with the Holy Spirit and began to speak in different tongues, as the Spirit enabled them to proclaim …. at this sound, they gathered in a large crowd, but they were confused because each one heard them speaking in his own language. They were astounded, and in amazement they asked, 'Are not all these people who are speaking Galileans? Then how does each of us hear them in his own native language?'" (Acts 2:1–8).

The Father, Son, and Holy Spirit

*Jesus speaks of the relationship of love that unites him to the Father, but also of the Spirit with whom he is one. God wants us to enter into this relationship, too. To express this, Christians speak of the Trinitarian God, One God in Three Divine Persons—God the Father, God the Son, and God the Holy Spirit. An icon helps us to imagine this mystery. In the icon of the **Hospitality of Abraham**, Christians see the three angels as an image of the Trinity.*

What is the Trinity?

In the Gospels, Jesus does not speak directly of the Trinity. He speaks of his Father and the Spirit, and he presents himself as the Son. Only gradually will the first generations of Christians speak of the Trinity as a way to explain that God the Father, God the Son, and God the Holy Spirit who is revealed in Jesus are Three Divine Persons in One God.

This icon was created between 1425 and 1427 by the Russian monk Andrei Rublev. The original is exhibited in Moscow. It represents an episode in the Bible: the visit of three strangers to Abraham and his wife Sarah (Genesis 18:1–22). In this story, Abraham addresses one person, the "Lord," but he also sees three people. When Rublev lived, Eastern tradition represented God this way to express the mystery of the Trinity. Christians see these three people as the Father on the left, the Son in the center, and the Holy Spirit on the right. These three characters have the same face but not the same posture. The Father sits straight because he is the origin of everything. The Son and the Spirit are leaning toward the Father, and their right hands express humility because they receive their mission from the Father. The icon presents a sense of peace and harmony (read more about this icon on page 15).

The three angels are pictured in a circle. The left angel represents God the Father. He blesses the cup and passes it to the central angel. At the center is the hand of the central angel, representing Jesus. He wears a red robe with a gold cloth on his shoulder, signs of his kingship.

The Spirit wears a green robe, the color of life, because the Spirit is the one who gives life.

Each holds a staff, as a symbol of power.

Pictures and names to talk about the Spirit

Breath, wind, devouring fire, water ... The Bible is full of varied images to evoke the presence of the Holy Spirit throughout history. These are more than just simple symbols; they help us understand who the Holy Spirit is and what the Spirit's presence can do in our lives.

THE BREATH

In the Bible we find the Hebrew word *ruah* which means "breath." Breath is what animates the body. We cannot live without breathing, and we die when it expires. In Genesis, it is written that this breath of life comes from God and returns to God at our death. In the Gospel of John, when the Risen Jesus manifests himself to his Apostles, he breathes on them and says, "Receive the Holy Spirit" (John 20:22).

THE WIND

It makes trees bend, destroys houses and capsizes ships (see Ezekiel 13:13; 27:26), but it can also be like a refreshing breeze and a gentle murmur (see 1 Kings 19:12). It dries up the soil but also waters it so that life can emerge (see 1 Kings 18:45). We cannot lock up the wind or store it. It is elusive.

Jesus said to Nicodemus: "The wind blows where it wills, and you can hear the sound it makes, but you do not know where it comes from or where it goes; so it is with everyone who is born of the Spirit" (John 3:8).

On the day of Pentecost, the Apostles were gathered together, "and suddenly there came from the sky a noise like a strong driving wind, and it filled the entire house in which they were" (Acts 2:2).

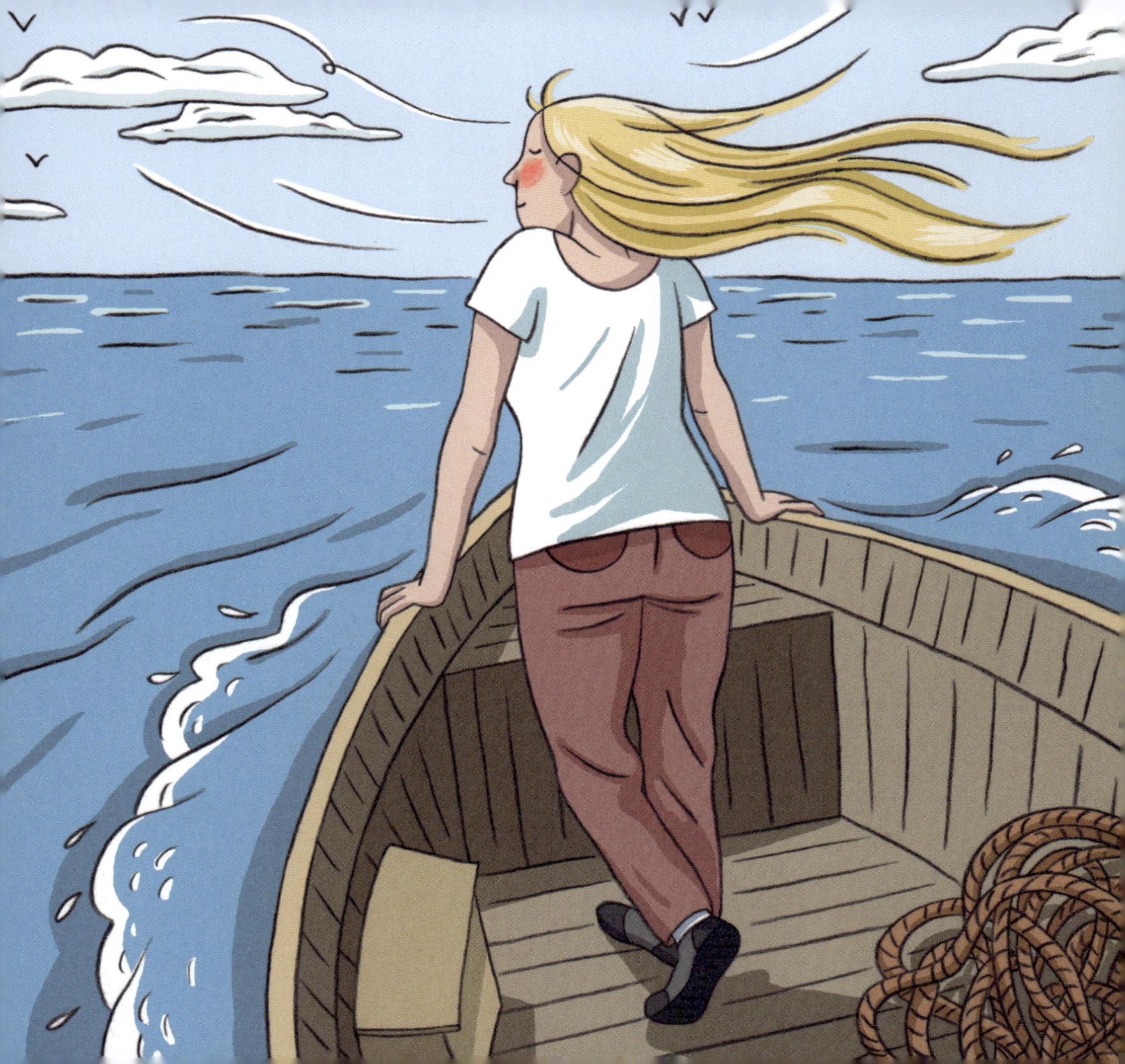

FIRE

In the Bible, fire illuminates, warms, and ignites. It also purifies things such as precious metals. The Spirit is a fire that cleanses and renews us from the inside.

John the Baptist says of Jesus: "He will baptize you with the Holy Spirit and Fire" (Matthew 3:11).

The promise is fulfilled at Pentecost: "Then there appeared to them tongues as of fire. And they were all filled with the Holy Spirit" (Acts 2:3–4).

WATER, THE REFRESHING SOURCE

Water is the symbol of life, and the Spirit is the one who brings life to us. The Spirit is like water, preventing our hearts from drying up and hardening, but we need to allow the Spirit to create channels within us so that we can grow with strength. Finally, the Spirit is the water that allows us to bear fruit like a tree. God says, "I will pour out water upon the thirsty ground, streams upon the dry land; I will pour out my spirit upon your offspring."(Isaiah 44:3).

Jesus said, "Let anyone who thirsts come to me and drink. Whoever believes in me, as scripture says: 'Rivers of living water will flow from within him'" (John 7:37–39).

Advocate or Paraclete

Paraclete comes from the Greek paracletos which means "lawyer." The paraclete is the one who asks, prays, consoles, encourages, and defends. The Holy Spirit that Jesus promises to send to his disciples is really a person, not just a force. The Spirit acts for us, consoles us, and defends us against enemies, and at the same time helps us act according to the will of Jesus Christ.

Jesus says: "The Advocate, the Holy Spirit that the Father will send in my name—he will teach you everything and remind you of all that [I] told you" (John 14:26).

"When the Advocate comes whom I will send you from the Father, the Spirit of truth that proceeds from the Father, he will testify to me. And you also testify, because you have been with me from the beginning" (John 15:26-27).

THE DOVE

Doves are beautiful, calm birds that move silently, without being noticed. In the same way, the Holy Spirit is a silent friend who accompanies us always. Even when we are by ourselves, we are never alone. Doves are associated with the Spirit because they are a symbol of peace, and peace is one of the Gifts of the Holy Spirit.

"After Jesus was baptized, he came up from the water and behold, the heavens were opened [for him], and he saw the Spirit of God descending like a dove [and] coming upon him" (Matthew 3:16).

THE LIGHT AND THE CLOUD

In the Old Testament, God's appearance was often accompanied by an illuminated cloud. This was also a sign of the Spirit: "On the seventh day (the Lord) called Moses from the midst of the cloud" (Exodus 24:16).

"As Moses entered the tent, the column of cloud would come down and stand at its entrance while the Lord spoke with Moses" (Exodus 33:9).

In the New Testament, Saint Luke describes the Transfiguration: "While he (Peter) was still speaking, a cloud came and cast a shadow over them, and they became frightened when they entered the cloud. Then from the cloud came a voice that said, 'This is my chosen Son; listen to him'" (Luke 9:34–35).

At Jesus's Ascension to his Father, the Apostles watch him disappear in a cloud (Luke 1:9). It is also prophesied that that Jesus will return to earth in a cloud: "And then they will see the Son of Man coming in a cloud with power and great glory" (Luke 21:27).

Comforter

The word comforter is another translation of the word "paracletos." The Holy Spirit comforts us in our trials, helping us to see our faults clearly, but also comforting us by helping us understand that we are forgiven. In painful or distressing situations, the Spirit provides great peace and the trust in God that nothing can change his love for us.

ANOINTING WITH OIL

In the Old Testament, anointing with oil is the sign that a person is consecrated for a specific mission and that God is sending the assistance of the Holy Spirit. Oil goes into the skin and stays there. The Holy Spirit is like oil, leaving a permanent imprint in us.

In the Book of Isaiah we read: "The spirit of the Lord God is upon me, because the Lord has anointed me" (Isaiah 61:1). Jesus repeats this phrase in the Gospel of Luke (4:18).

In speaking of the Holy Spirit, John says: "The anointing that you received from him remains in you, so that you do not need anyone to teach you. But his anointing teaches you about everything" (1 John 2:27).

LAYING ON OF HANDS

In the Bible, hands heal and call the Holy Spirit. Jesus heals by laying on his hands. Afterward, his Apostles do the same thing. It is also by this laying on of hands that they give the Holy Spirit; thus Peter and John pray that the Samaritans receive the Holy Spirit. "For it had not yet fallen upon any of them; they had only been baptized in the name of the Lord Jesus. Then they laid hands on them and they received the Holy Spirit" (Acts 8:16–17).

Spirit of truth

The Spirit's role is to help us understand who Christ is, not only with our minds but with our hearts. Jesus says the Sprit helps us understand what he says about his Father. The Spirit is also called the "Spirit of truth" because as we look honestly at everything that goes wrong in our lives, the inspiration of the Spirit guides us to the truth.

"But when he comes, the Spirit of truth, he will guide you to all truth. He will not speak on his own, but he will speak what he hears, and will declare to you the things that are coming" (John 16:13).

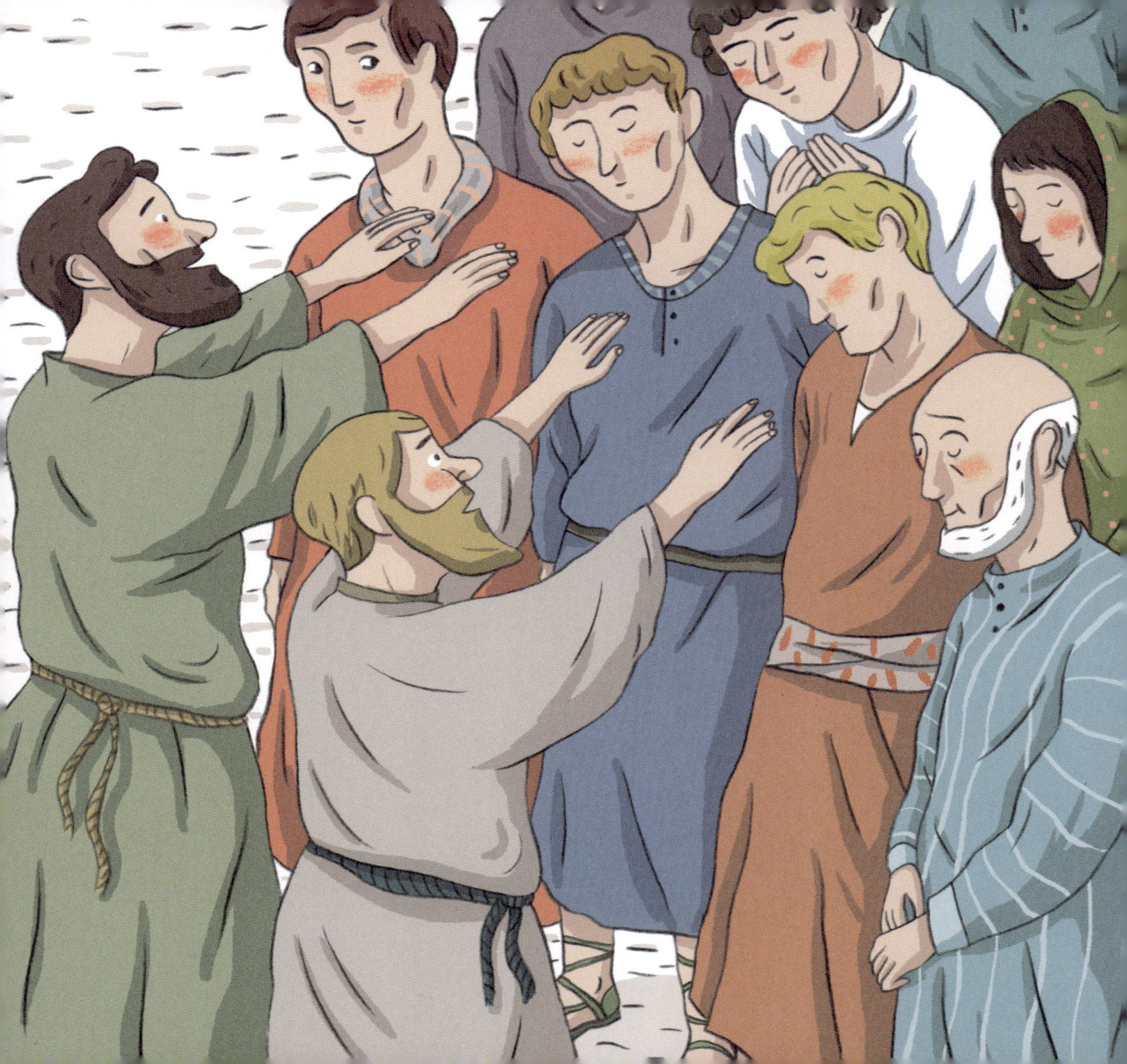

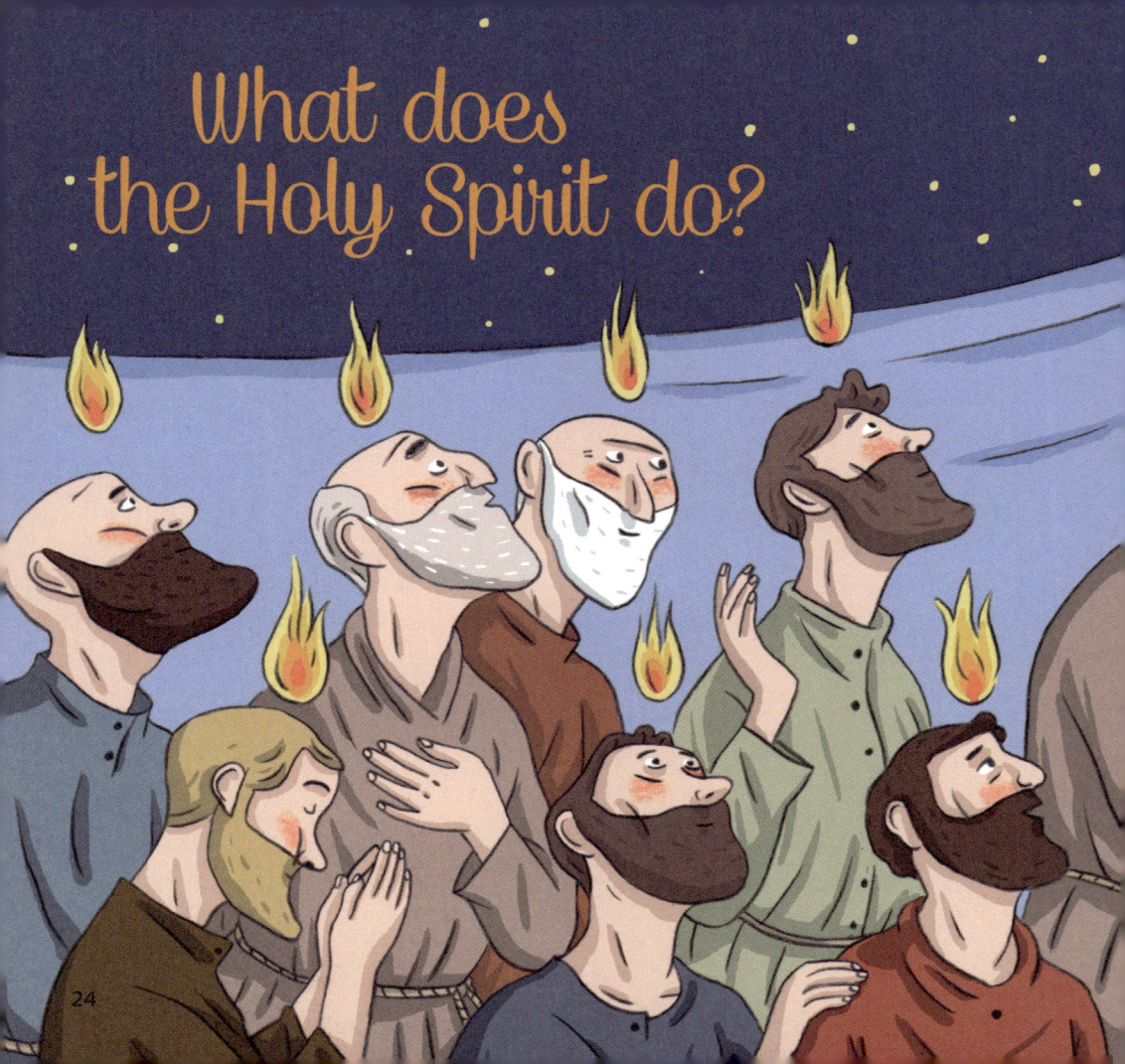

What does the Holy Spirit do?

25

The Seven Gifts of the Holy Spirit

In the Church's tradition, the Holy Spirit gives seven gifts: wisdom, understanding, counsel, fortitude, knowledge, piety, and fear of the Lord*. The number seven symbolizes totality, but the list of the seven gifts is not final! When we receive the Spirit, we are filled with these gifts, but that does not mean that we have them once and for all. Rather, they are areas in which we are invited to keep improving all our life.

WHERE DO THESE SEVEN GIFTS COME FROM?

In the Old Testament, in a passage from the Book of Isaiah, it is written, "But a shoot shall sprout from the stump of Jesse, and from his roots a bud shall blossom. The spirit of the Lord shall rest upon him: a spirit of wisdom and of understanding, a spirit of counsel and of strength, a spirit of knowledge and of fear of the Lord, and his delight shall be the fear of the Lord" (Isaiah 11:1–3). In rereading this text, Christians attributed these gifts to Jesus Christ, the Messiah expected by Israelites, and finally, to the Holy Spirit.

WHAT ARE THE GIFTS FOR?

As all gifts are free, the Gifts of the Spirit are freely offered to us so that we can become closer to God. In his Epistles (letters), Saint Paul speaks of these spiritual gifts: to serve, teach, encourage, direct, sympathize, evangelize ... When we receive the Holy Spirit, each of us is filled with gifts, not to keep for ourselves, but to use for others. When we exercise these gifts, the Spirit acts through us to enrich the Church and transform the world.

* The fear of the Lord is a feeling of respect for the greatness of God that goes beyond our imagination. When we fear God, we want to be faithful in all areas of our life.

In this traditional image of Jesse's tree, a tree representing his offspring comes out of Jesse's chest. It culminates with Mary and Jesus. Around them, we find the great kings of Israel. Sometimes these kings are replaced by the seven Gifts of the Holy Spirit.

Charisms

*The Spirit has many ways to appear in people's lives, and each person's path is unique.
Saint Paul tells how, in the first communities of Christians, the Holy Spirit came to life through charisms, particular gifts that Christians received to increase the faith of communities.*

WHAT IS A *CHARISM*?

The word *charism* comes from the Greek *charisma*, meaning "free gift." In his Epistles, Saint Paul explains what these charisms are and what they serve: "To each individual the manifestation of the Spirit is given for some benefit. To one is given through the Spirit the expression of wisdom; to another the expression of knowledge according to the same Spirit; to another faith by the same Spirit; to another gifts of healing by the one Spirit; to another mighty deeds; to another prophecy; to another discernment of spirits; to another varieties of tongues; to another interpretation of tongues. But one and the same Spirit produces all of these, distributing them individually to each person as he wishes" (1 Corinthans 12:7–11). Saint Paul classifies them according to their importance. The most important is "charity." Today we would call it "love." Even though they are very visible and sometimes spectacular, the charisms are only one manifestation of the power of the Holy Spirit.

Charismatic Communities

The word charismatic is used to describe the communities that sprang up around 1960 from Protestant movements such as Pentecostalism.

The Catholic Church also desires to see a "new Pentecost" by encouraging people to be attentive to the Holy Spirit in their lives.

There are charismatic communities in the Catholic Church, too, in which people experience "the outpouring of the Spirit" or "baptism in the Spirit." People have different responses to this "outpouring of the Spirit." Some people fall asleep, feeling very calm. Others cry, or have a feeling of warmth. Some say that they have had the overwhelming experience of feeling infinitely loved by God, resulting in a sense of peace and deep joy. Some don't feel anything different but believe that the Spirit is still powerfully present.

PROPHECY AND DISCERNMENT

Prophets speak in the name of God, but the prophecy must always be verified and interpreted by a person who has received the charism of "discernment of spirits." It is a question of knowing if what has been said comes from the Holy Spirit or the person's own spirit or even a bad spirit. Saint Paul says, "Two or three prophets should speak, and the others discern" (1 Corinthians 14:29).

HEALING

Jesus heals the sick with the power of the Holy Spirit. But healings are not an end in themselves; they are there to support the announcement of the Good News. Thus, to the scribes who reproached him for forgiving sins, Jesus answered: "Which is easier, to say to the paralytic, 'Your sins are forgiven,' or to say, 'Rise, pick up your mat and walk.'"

"But that you may know that the Son of Man has authority to forgive sins on earth"—he said to the paralytic, 'I say to you, rise, pick up your mat, and go home.' He rose, picked up his mat at once, and went away in the sight of everyone" (Mark 2:9–12).

MIRACLES

Jesus explained that he performed miracles through the presence of the Holy Spirit: "The Spirit of the Lord is upon me, because he has anointed me to bring glad tidings to the poor. He has sent me to proclaim liberty to captives and recovery of sight to the blind, to let the oppressed go free" (Luke 4:18). Similarly, his Apostles received the Spirit and performed miracles: "Many signs and wonders were done among the people at the hands of the Apostles" (Acts 5:12).

THE GIFT OF TONGUES AND THE GIFT OF INTERPRETATION

These charisms are evoked by Saint Paul in his letters: "To another mighty deeds; to another prophecy; to another discernment of spirits; to another varieties of tongues; to another interpretation of tongues. But one and the same Spirit produces all of these, distributing them individually to each person as he wishes" (1 Corinthians 12:10-11). Today, in some prayer groups, people pray to experience the charisms evoked by Saint Paul.

THE TEACHING GIFT

The one who receives this charism understands the heart of the Word of God and knows how to share it with others so that it lives in them.

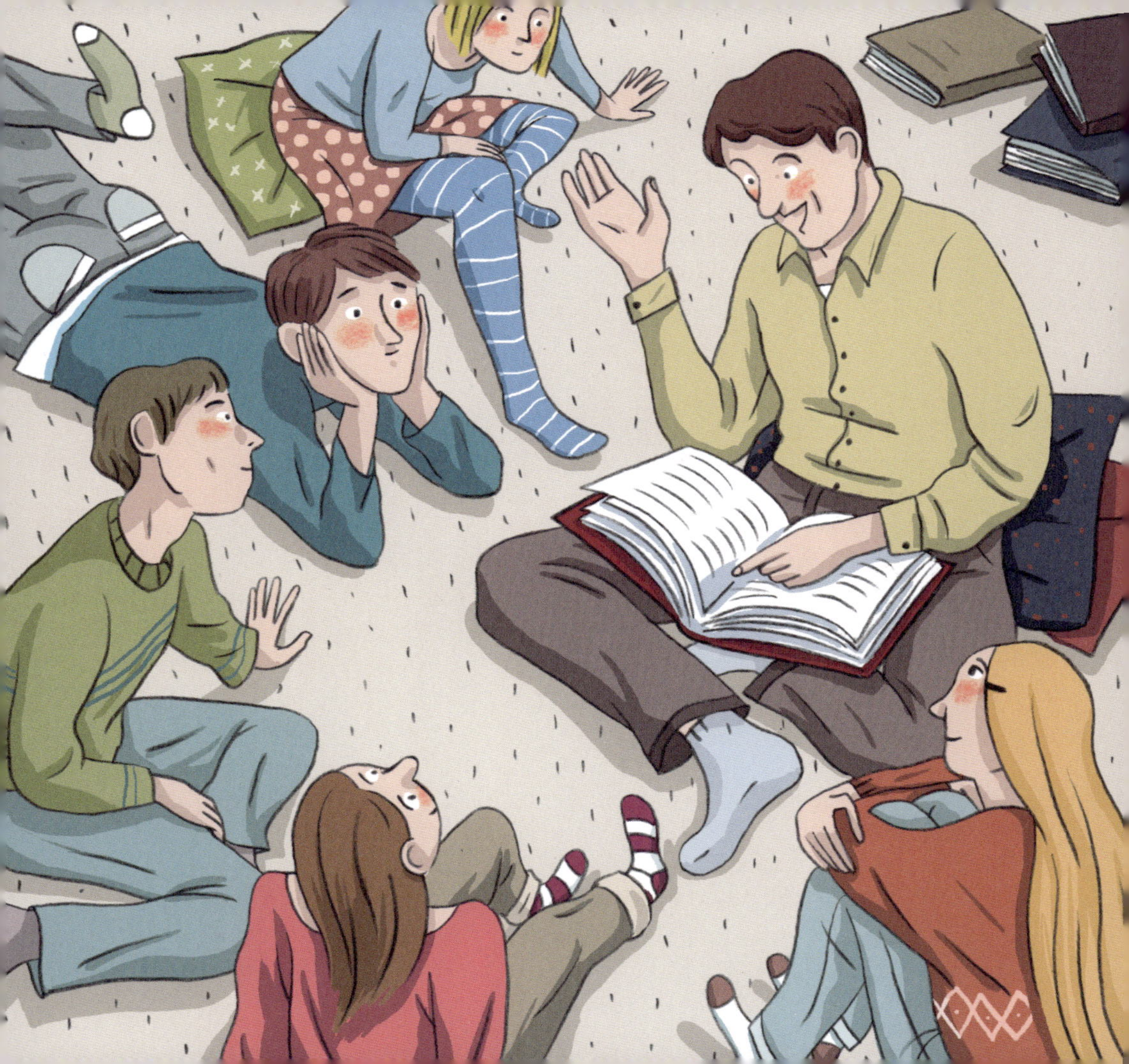

The Holy Spirit leads us to love and forgiveness

The most precious gift that the Spirit gives us is love. Saint Paul places it above all the other gifts and charisms. He calls this love "charity." God loves us with this kind of love so that we are able to love ourselves and others. It is like a torrent of water that cannot be restrained; it goes through us and over us.

THE SPIRIT IS LOVE

The Bible explains that the Holy Spirit and the love of God are linked: "The love of God has been poured out into our hearts through the Holy Spirit that has been given to us" (Romans 5:5).

"If we love one another, God remains in us, and his love is brought to perfection in us. This is how we know that we remain in him and he in us, that he has given us of his Spirit" (1 John 4:12–13).

We can also rely on the testimony of those who have experienced the Spirit in their lives: they say they feel that they are deeply loved by God. And that gives them a lot of joy and peace.

THE SPIRIT MAKES US LOVE

The Spirit communicates to our soul that God loves us. If we know that we are loved by God, we can not keep this love for ourselves. The Holy Spirit awakens the love of God and of our neighbor in our heart and teaches us how to love. The Spirit pushes us out of our selfishness so that we can forgive what is difficult to forgive and battle injustice. John says, "As for you, the anointing that you received from him remains in you, so that you do not need anyone to teach you. But his anointing teaches you about everything and is true and not false; just as it taught you, remain in him" (1 John 2:27). So when we fail to love or forgive, we can always ask the Holy Spirit to help us by instilling in us the desire to love and forgive.

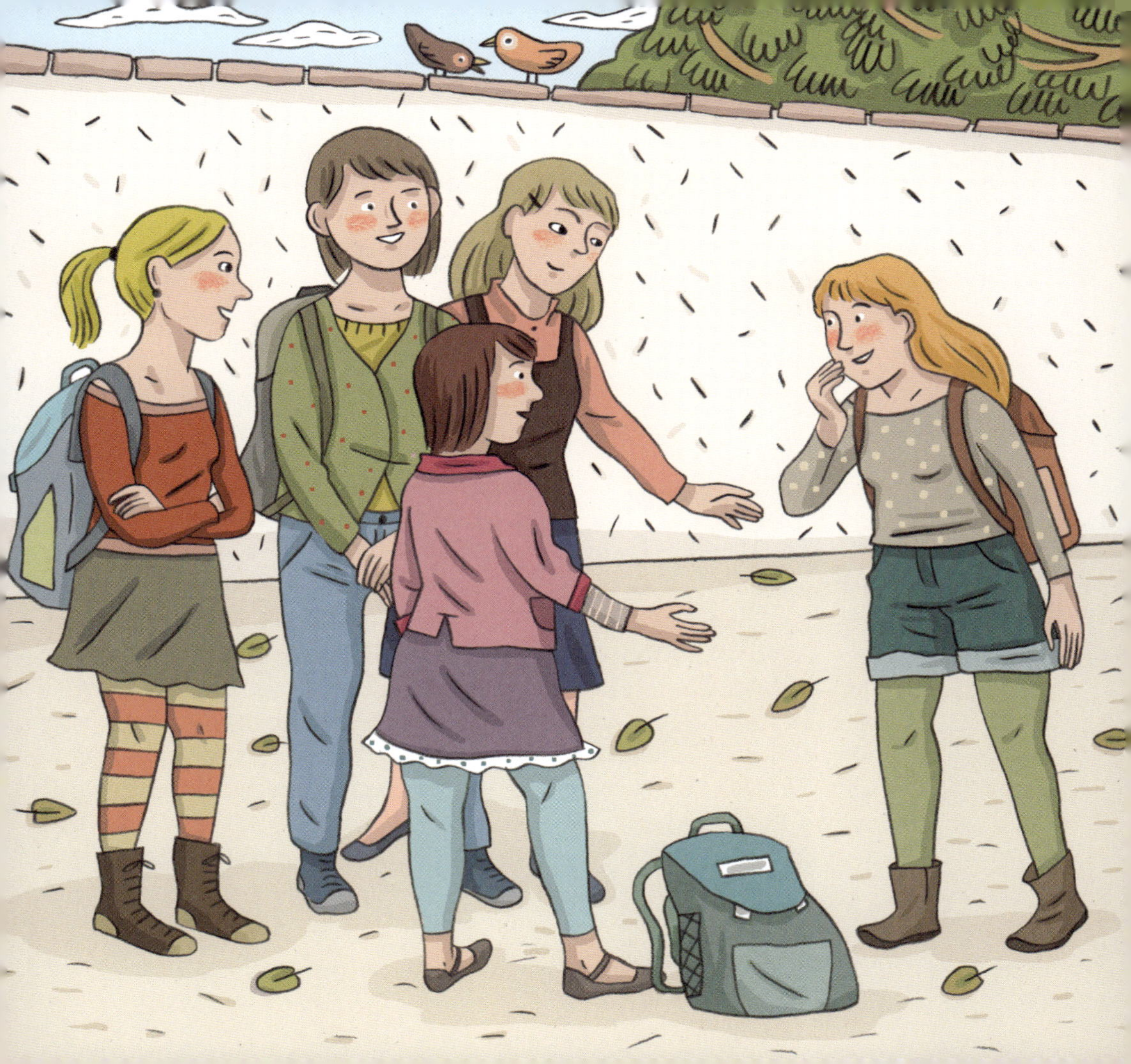

We are "Children of God"

We all pray with the prayer that begins with "Our Father." Yet we do not always realize what it means to be a child of God, able to call God "Father." The Holy Spirit helps us understand how special this is.

GOD IS SO IMMENSE AND YET ALSO AS CLOSE AS A LOVING PARENT

In the Old Testament, God is called "Lord," "Almighty God" but also "Father." Jesus goes even further: under the action of the Holy Spirit, he uses a very familiar word for addressing God. He calls God *abba*, which means "dad." This shocked the people around him. Jesus teaches us that we too can address God as a father. That is why he teaches his Apostles the prayer that begins with "Our Father."

THE SPIRIT SPEAKS TO OUR SPIRIT

Hearing Jesus say "dad" or saying the "Our Father" is not enough, however, to make us feel like "children of God." It is the Spirit that brings this to life in our hearts, as Saint Paul explains to us: "For you did not receive a spirit of slavery to fall back into fear, but you received a spirit of adoption, through which we cry, 'Abba, Father!' The Spirit itself bears witness with our spirit that we are children of God" (Romans 8:15–16). The Holy Spirit helps us to turn to the Father in prayer, teaching us to speak to the Father with the confidence of a child.

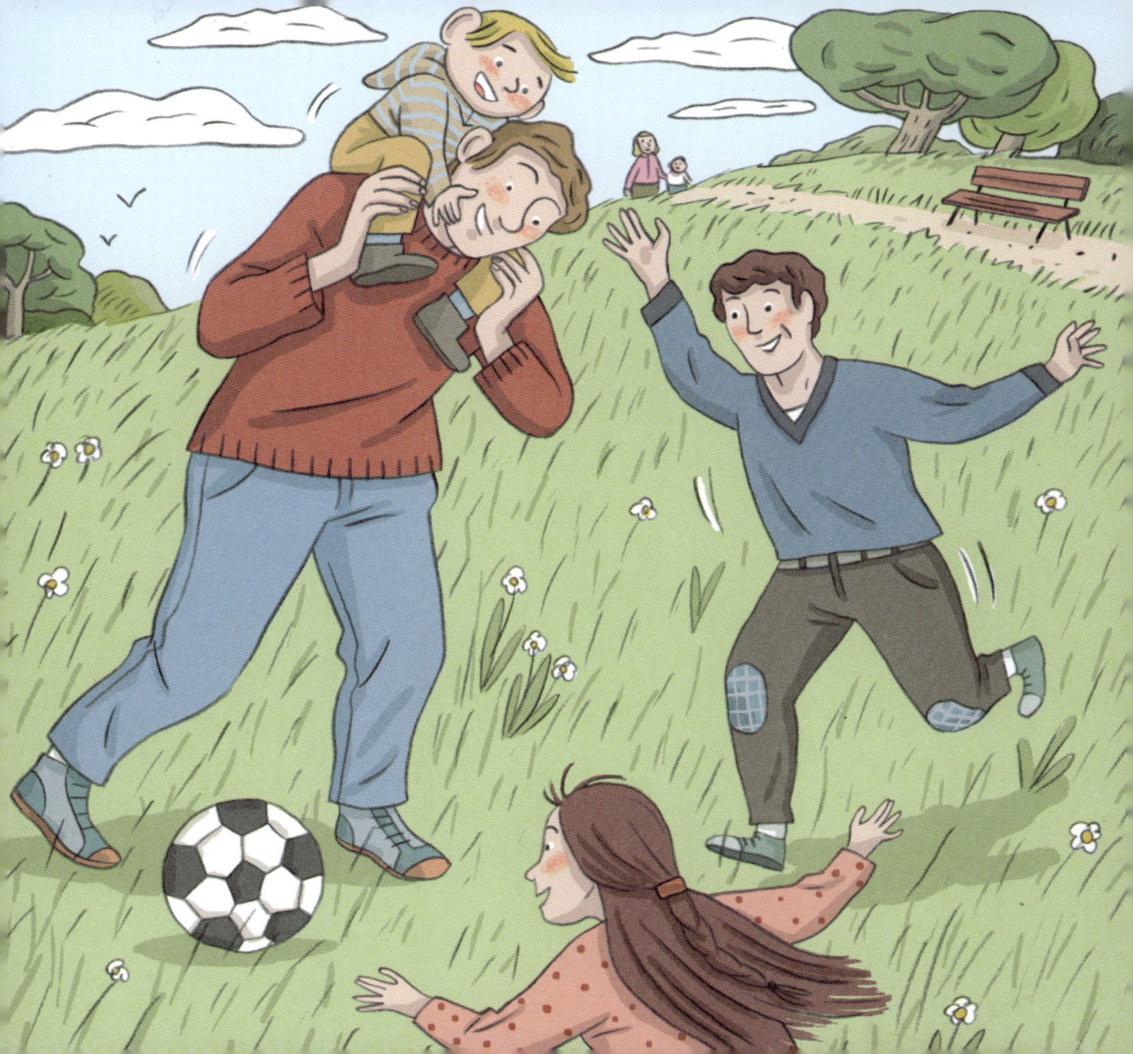

Receive the Holy Spirit

37

Baptism:
Born of the Spirit

Baptism is the sacrament which forgives Original Sin and makes us members of the Church. The person who is baptized is buried with Christ to be raised to a new life with him. The person receives the Holy Spirit, who will guide this new life.

BORN AGAIN

In the Gospels, Jesus meets a very devout Jewish person named Nicodemus. Jesus tells him that no one can see the reign of God unless he is reborn. Nicodemus asks him: "How is it possible to be born when one is already old? Can we get into the womb of his mother to be born a second time?" Jesus gives him this answer: "Amen, amen, I say to you, no one can enter the kingdom of God without being born of water and Spirit. What is born of flesh is flesh and what is born of spirit is spirit" (John 3:5-6).

Thus, in Baptism, the Holy Spirit acts to bring us into a new dimension, a spiritual life animated and guided by the Spirit. The Holy Spirit fills all who are baptized and unites them to one another. Together they form what is called the big family of Christians, the Church.

SIGNS OF THE PRESENCE OF THE SPIRIT

At Baptism, the priest or deacon places his hands on the person being baptized to call the Holy Spirit upon him or her. The baptized person then receives the strength to fight any kind of evil, both the evil that is inside the person and the evil that is outside of them. After this, the Spirit will dwell within the baptized person until death. The person becomes a "temple of the Spirit" (1 Corinthians 6:19). Then the priest or deacon places Sacred Chrism (holy oil) on the person's forehead. In the Bible, such an anointing calls the Spirit upon a person, enabling the person to serve God. Thus the baptized person is "anointed" to live according to the Gospel. He or she becomes the chosen one of God.

Confirmation: God renews his gifts

Today we celebrate Baptism and Confirmation at different times for practical and pastoral reasons, but in the early days of the Church, this distinction did not exist. The laying on of hands for the Gift of the Spirit was part of the rites of Baptism.

SACRAMENTS OF CHRISTIAN INITIATION

Baptism, Confirmation, and Eucharist are called Sacraments of Christian Initiation. Being "initiated" means introduced to a new kind of life Thus, these sacraments are the means to move through the stages of our Christian life. Through Baptism, we are reborn in the Holy Spirit and become members of Body of Christ. In Confirmation, we welcome the Holy Spirit who makes us more like Christ and witnesses of his Passion, Death, and Resurrection.

A LITTLE HISTORY

In the Acts of the Apostles, it is recorded that the Apostles laid hands on the newly baptized Gentiles so that they would receive the Spirit (Acts 8:15–17). Until the third century, Confirmation remained attached to Baptism because it was the bishop who did the baptizing and confirming. As baptisms became more and more numerous, the bishops entrusted Baptism to the priests and then also deacons, but reserved Confirmation for themselves. Thus, Confirmation gradually was separated from Baptism and became a sacrament in its own right, at least among Catholics.

Orthodox and Protestant Baptism

Among Orthodox Christians, Confirmation is given right after Baptism, as it was in the first centuries. It is called chrismation, a word that comes from the word "holy chrism," the scented oil used to anoint those entering the Church. Given at the same celebration as Baptism, the priest confirms the person by anointing him or her with Sacred Chrism on several parts of the body. The priest tells the person: "Receive the mark of the gift of the Holy Spirit." Then the newly baptized and confirmed person receives Communion for the first time, even if he or she is still a baby.

With Protestants, Confirmation isn't usually considered a sacrament. If it is, it is given to adolescents around the age of fourteen and marks the end of religious education.

An Orthodox Christian charismation

WHAT IS THE POINT OF BEING CONFIRMED?

Confirmation is sometimes called "Pentecost of the Christian." Indeed, when a person receives the anointing of Sacred Chrism during Confirmation, the same thing happens as did for the Apostles on the day of Pentecost (see Acts 2:1–13). Once a person receives the Holy Spirit, they are no longer afraid to announce the Good News to those they meet. They speak with confidence, and their hearts are filled with joy. They feel the strength and courage that comes from the Holy Spirit. They are empowered to go as fearless missionaries in unknown lands.

WHAT IS THE AGE OF CONFIRMATION?

For Catholics, the age for receiving Confirmation has evolved over the centuries. In earlier times, Confirmation was celebrated around age seven, before First Communion. Today, many people are confirmed in high school.

Adults who enter the Church are baptized and confirmed at the same celebration. But every diocese has its own rules. The only thing that does not vary is the order: Confirmation always comes after Baptism.

WHO CAN BE CONFIRMED?

The Church believes that Confirmation gives a particular strength, that of the Holy Spirit, so that those already baptized as Christians may lead a life faithful to the Gospel and to have the courage to witness to others. That is why, following a time of preparation, the Church welcomes anyone who has been baptized to receive the Sacrament of Confirmation.

WHY RECEIVE THE SPIRIT AGAIN WHEN WE HAVE ALREADY RECEIVED IT AT BAPTISM?

The Holy Spirit is not a magic force, but rather, the gift of God. And when God gives, his gifts are boundless. The Spirit is not something that appears and then disappears. God's Spirit is always present, and Confirmation strengthens our willingness to allow the Spirit to work within us.

PREPARING TO RECEIVE THE HOLY SPIRIT

This can be done in a group with other youth, or in a group of adults. We talk with others about what it means to follow Christ in our everyday lives, and discuss the choices and commitments that entails. Sometimes, at the end of the preparation, each candidate writes a personal letter to the bishop in which they explain why he or she desires to receive Confirmation.

HOW DO YOU KNOW IF YOU ARE READY?

Ask yourself some questions: Am I a Christian by personal choice rather than simply trying to please my parents or to fit in with my friends? Am I willing to be a witness of Jesus Christ through my life and my actions? If you can answer "yes" to these questions, you are ready.

THE CELEBRATION OF CONFIRMATION INCLUDES FOUR HIGHLIGHTS:

▶ *The call*
Each confirmand (person being confirmed) is called by the bishop or his delegate by his or her name. The person responds by standing up or moving forward. This shows a personal desire to receive the sacrament.

▶ *The profession of faith*
Confirmands reaffirm the faith of the Church as their parents did for them when they were little children. They answer "I do" to each question the bishop asks.

▶ *The laying on of hands*
The bishop lays hands on those who will be confirmed in order for the Holy Spirit to come upon them. The bishop says a prayer that mentions the Seven Gifts of the Spirit that the confirmands will receive: wisdom, understanding, counsel, fortitude, knowledge, piety, and fear of the Lord.

▶ *The anointing with Sacred Chrism*

The bishop makes a cross with Sacred Chrism (holy oil) on the forehead of the confirmand. He says, "Be sealed with the Gift of the Holy Spirit." The confirmand responds, "Amen." This oil penetrates the skin and signifies how the Holy Spirit enters the heart of the Christian to dwell there.

Sacred Chrism

Sacred Chrism is a mixture of olive oil and balm, which has a very pleasant fragrance. It represents how the Holy Spirit enters the life of the Christian so that the joy and peace of the Lord can be seen and felt. The baptized and the confirmed are called to be "the aroma of Christ for God among those who are being saved and among those who are perishing" (2 Corinthians 2:15). This oil is consecrated by the bishop during the Chrism Mass that takes place once a year, during Holy Week.

AFTER CONFIRMATION ...

We Christians have great hope. We know that God loves us and that Christ accompanies us and gives us his Spirit. Filled with the Holy Spirit, we, like the disciples, can announce this Good News. We are invited to do it first by the way we act toward others. People around us will ask if our way of life is a testimony of this hope, and they will wonder where it comes from. God acts through our speech, our gestures, our eyes.

Sometimes we will have to give witness with our words. For that, we must be ready.

Peter says, "You must always be ready to explain to those who ask you to give an account of the hope that is in you." And he adds, "But do it with gentleness and respect" (1 Peter 3:15–16). It's not about trying to convince others at all costs, but to start listening to those who seek the truth and offering them the opportunity to meet Jesus. This can be done by a simple testimony of how we ourselves met Jesus Christ. Finally, we need to ask the Holy Spirit to act in our lives by putting the right words on our lips and preparing the hearts of those who hear us.

In other sacraments

Confirmation is the sacrament of the Gift of the Spirit, but the Holy Spirit is present in all the sacraments. It is through the Spirit that the priest is ordained, celebrates Mass, forgives sins, and gives comfort to the sick.

ANOINTING OF THE SICK

In earlier times, *Anointing of the Sick* was given only to dying people and was called *Extreme Unction* or "last rites." Today, this sacrament can be given to anyone suffering from a long physical or mental illness who asks for it. During Mass or privately, the priest anoints the person with holy oil called the Oil of the Infirm.

Because a sick person may feel helpless or lose hope in God, the Sacrament of the Anointing of the Sick is the sign of the Holy Spirit who gives the strength and peace of God to go through the time of being sick. The sick person responds by putting his or her life in God's hands. The Apostle James says, "Is anyone among you sick? He should summon the presbyters of the church, and they should pray over him and anoint [him] with oil in the name of the Lord, and the prayer of faith will save the sick person, and the Lord will raise him up. If he has committed any sins, he will be forgiven" (James 5:14–15).

Holy Orders

A baptized man becomes a priest, a deacon, or a bishop through the Sacrament of Holy Orders. The laying on of hands and the anointing of Sacred Chrism, two signs of the Spirit, are found again in this sacrament. During an ordination, the future priest prostrates himself totally (lies flat) on the ground. Then the bishop and any other priests who are present lay their hands on him and say a prayer that calls the Holy Spirit to come upon the one being ordained. This gesture conveys to the priest the responsibility of a leading community and welcomes him into the community formed by all priests.

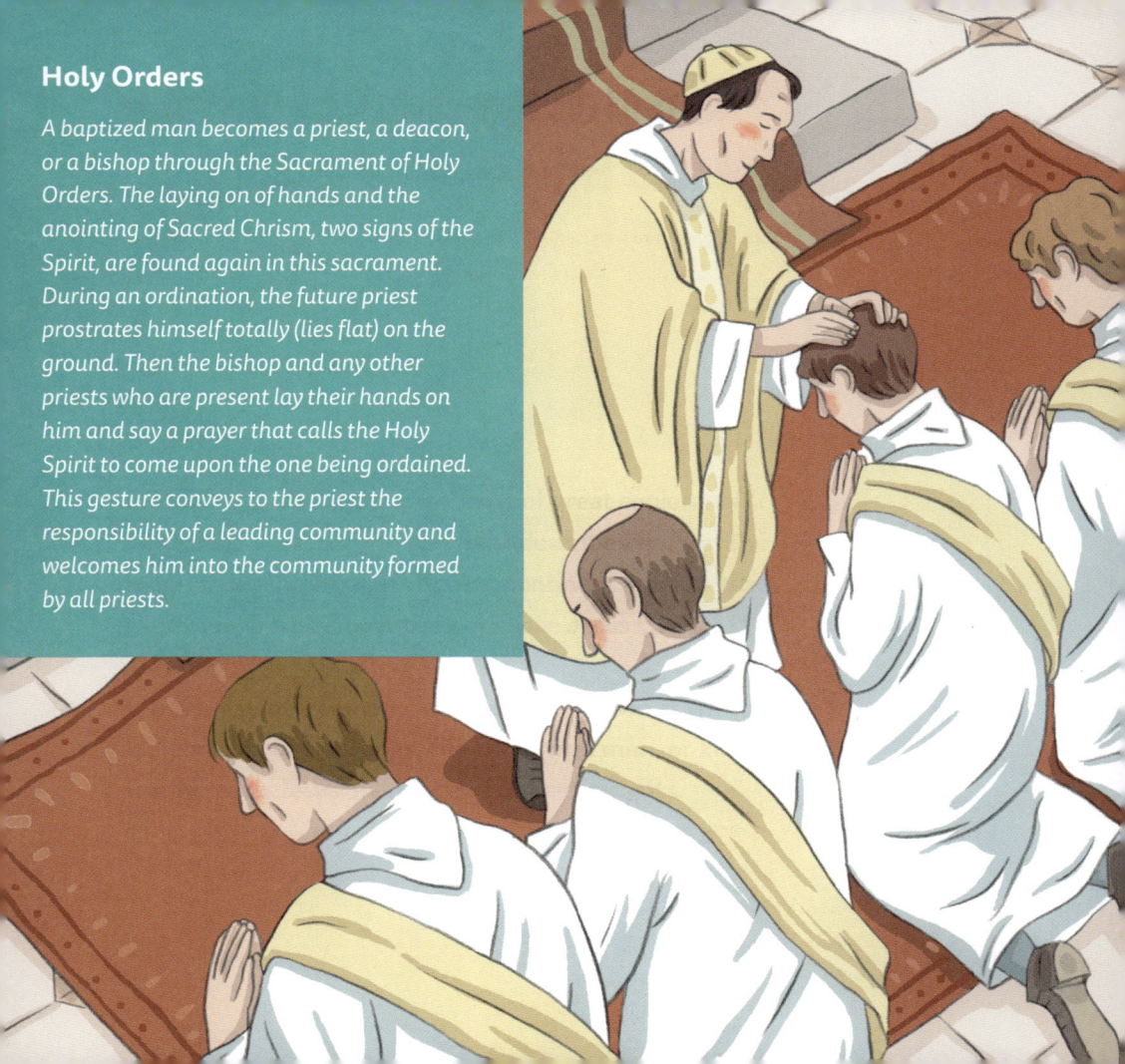

The Mass and the Eucharist

For many Catholics, the Holy Spirit can be somewhat difficult to understand. However, when we are gathered together as Church, the Holy Spirit is present. The Holy Spirit was at the beginning of the Church and is with us now. Through the Spirit, we receive the gift of Jesus' new life. At Mass, we try to open our hearts so that the Holy Spirit can act in us.

THE SIGN OF THE CROSS

"In the name of the Father, the Son and the Holy Spirit." In making the Sign of the Cross, we express the heart of our Christian faith: Jesus died on the Cross and is risen. We repeat that we believe in a Trinitarian God.

THE PRIEST ACTS THROUGH THE SPIRIT

When the priest says, "The Lord be with you," we answer "And with your spirit." This exchange means that as we celebrate the sacraments, we welcome the Spirit of the Lord. It is by the power of the Holy Spirit that the priest consecrates bread and wine so that they become the Body and Blood of Christ.

THE SPIRIT UNITES US IN THE GREAT EUCHARISTIC PRAYER OF THE MASS

The priest asks the Holy Spirit to gather us into one body, and his prayer ends with: "Through him, and with him, and in him, O God, almighty Father, in the unity of the Holy Spirit, all glory and honor is yours, for ever and ever." The Spirit unites us to others in Christ. This is what Jesus desires for us with all his heart: "So that they may all be one, as you, Father, are in me and I in you" (John 17:21). He spoke these words the night before he died on the Cross.

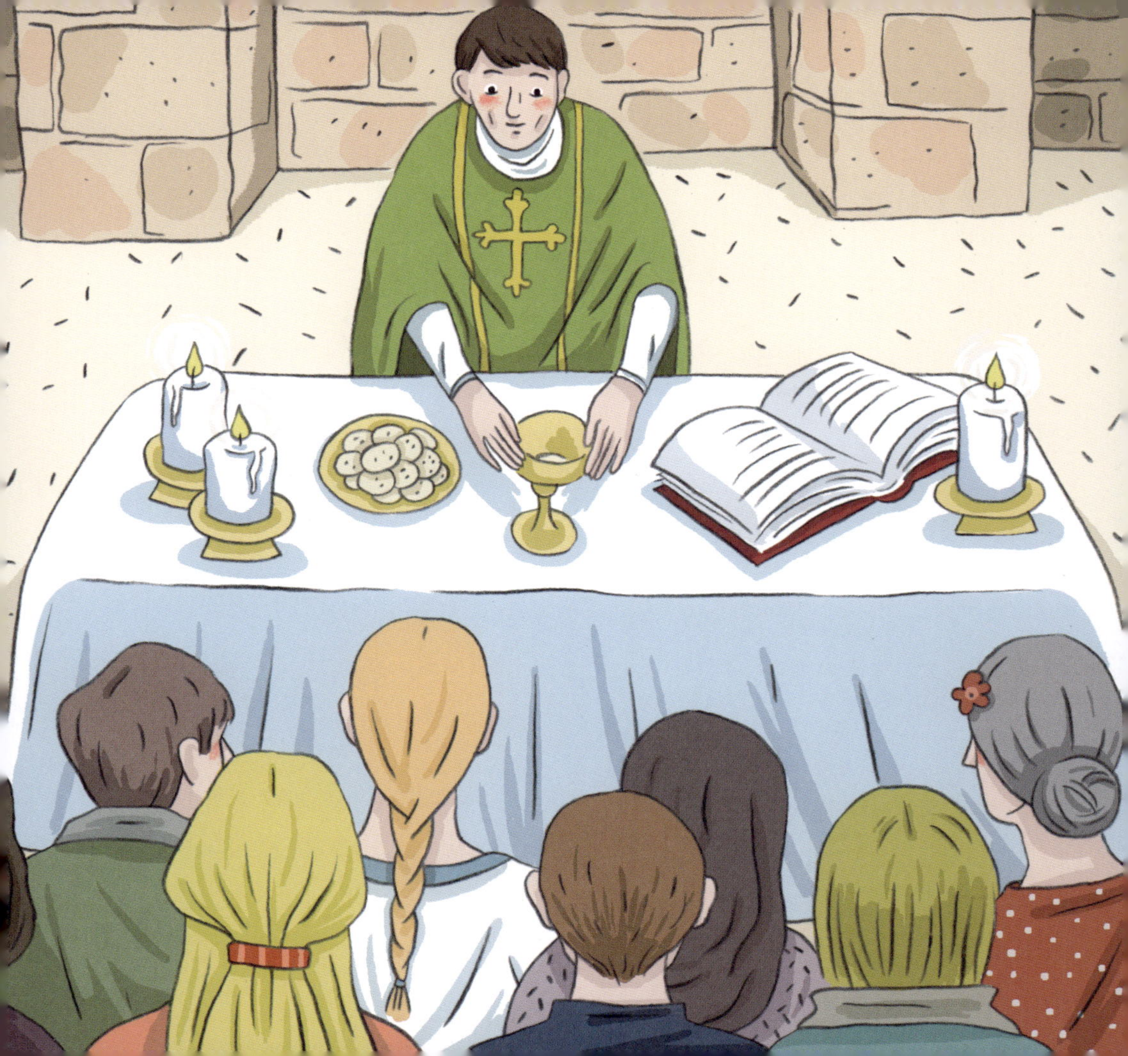

Living According to the Holy Spirit

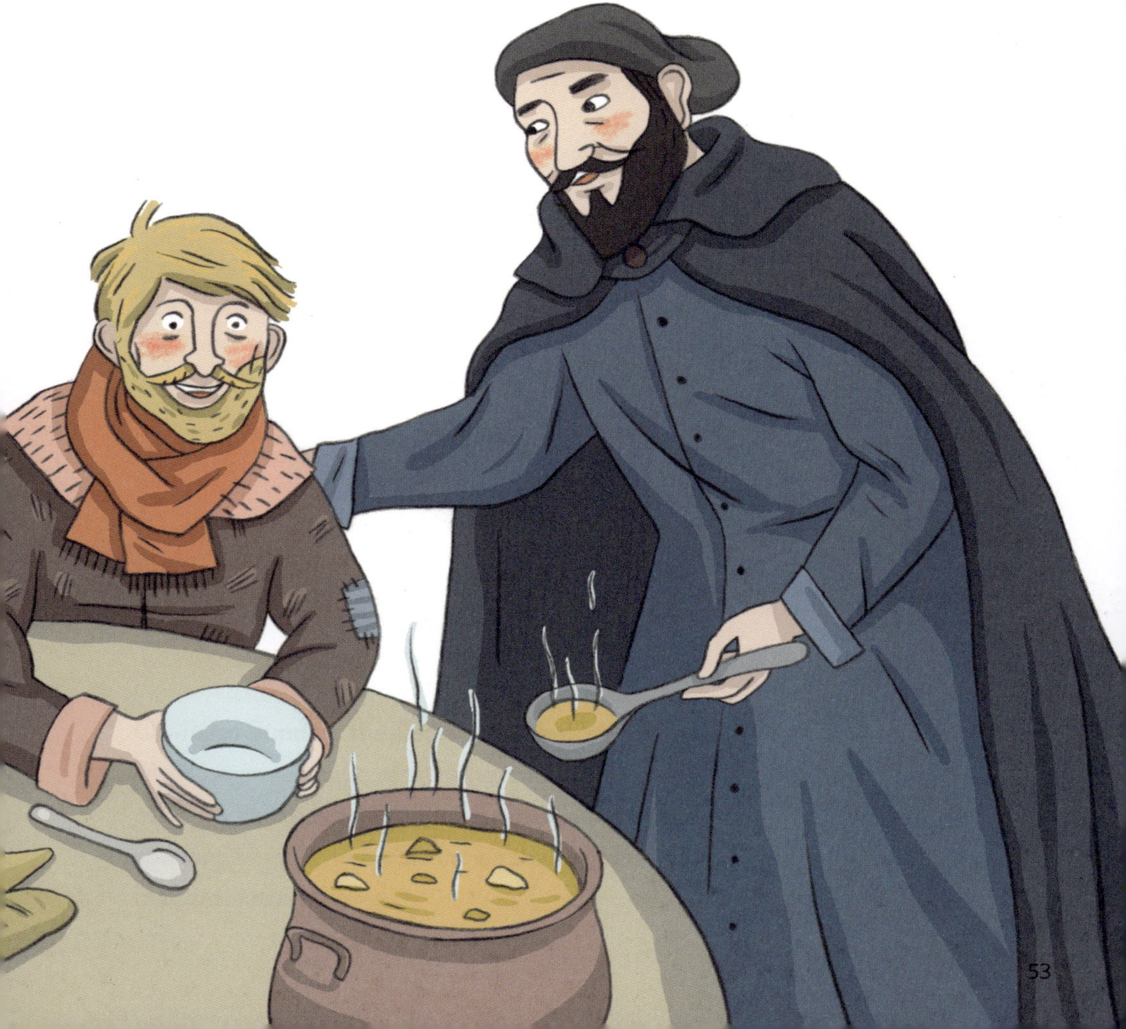

How do you live according to the Spirit?

You have just been confirmed or you will soon be confirmed. You are called to change the way you live. You have received the Spirit of God, not to keep this gift for yourself, but so that your life can be transformed, so that it can radiate the love of God. But what is does it mean to live according to the Spirit?

In the Acts of the Apostles, Saint Paul compares the life according to the Spirit to the life according to the flesh. "To live according to the flesh" means to live for oneself. When we live by the Spirit, we try to follow Jesus Christ. A life lived according to the Spirit bears fruits: "Love, joy, peace, patience, kindness, generosity, faithfulness, gentleness, self-control" (Galatians 5:22).

HOW DO WE PRAY?

To live by the Spirit is to let Christ guide our lives. But how can this happen if we do not have a personal and intimate relationship with the Holy Spirit? This relationship or friendship is built in prayer. But how do we pray? Even the disciples wondered this: "Master, teach us to pray" (Luke 11:1).

Praying can be a moment very early in the morning, or later in the evening before bedtime, or anytime during the day. When you pray, simply acknowledge your desire to meet God. There is no need to plan what you will say or ask. Be open to any surprise, without wishing to direct your prayer. After that, ask to the Holy Spirit to give you the words to pray. Saint Paul knows how difficult it is to pray, but he also assures us that the Spirit comes to our aid (see Romans 8:26).

If you do not feel ready to pray, or if you run out of time, you can also "recite" a prayer you know, such as the Our Father or Hail Mary. Or, like the Eastern Christians, you can repeat in your heart this simple prayer: "Lord Jesus, Son of the living God, have mercy on me, a sinner!"

ARE YOU THIRSTY?

Jesus said to the crowds, "Let anyone who thirsts come to me and drink." (John 7:37). And John added, "He said this in reference to the Spirit" (John 7:39). Thus, ask yourself these questions: Do I want to progress in the faith? Do I have a desire to meet Jesus, to become closer to him? If you do not feel this need, ask to the Spirit to create this thirst in you.

IN PRAYER, BE POOR BEFORE GOD

To let the Holy Spirit live within you, you need to empty yourself of all your concerns as well as your pride. When we say we are better than others, our hearts are closed and the Holy Spirit can not act in us. Letting go of pride is not about belittling yourself or despising yourself. Not at all! In prayer before God, we stand in our proper place, neither too high nor too low. God knows our heart and sees us as we are; we don't need to play a role or pretend to be something we are not. Saying thank you to God for little things as well as for big things can help. When we recognize that we have nothing and that we receive everything from God, our hearts open wide, and we are receptive to the action of the Holy Spirit.

LET YOURSELF BE GUIDED

The more we let go, the more the Spirit can act in us. The Spirit pushes us to make bold decisions such as to give up expensive things or to do the right thing when it is unpopular. The Spirit does not guarantee us a quiet life without difficulties. Just look at the lives of early Christians like Paul and Peter in the Acts of the Apostles. The first thing the Holy Spirit does to us is to push us so that we can receive more and more.

How do you know that the Spirit is speaking to you?

A tree is recognized by its fruits. We discern that it is the Spirit who speaks to us by his signs, his fruits: "The fruit of the Spirit is love, joy, peace, patience, kindness, generosity, faithfulness, gentleness, self-control" (Galatians 5:22–23). If a word or a thought that you received during your prayer brings you joy and peace, it probably comes from the Spirit. On the other hand, if what you receive disturbs you, worries you, or makes you feel guilty, you can be sure that it does not come from the Spirit.

Pray with others and ask for advice. In prayer, you can have returning thoughts or even intuitions. You may wonder if you are making these up. We need to check with other Christians to determine if what we hear in prayer comes from the Spirit. That's why the disciples, after meeting the Risen Jesus, went to share the news with others for them to confirm that it was not their imagination. Praying with others can also help you.

Obstacles to the action of the Spirit

DO NOT BE AFRAID!

When we read the story of Pentecost, we may fear that the Spirit will push us to do strange things. And what if we pray to the Holy Spirit and he asks us to do things that seem difficult or even impossible?

Do not be afraid. You are completely free when you respond to God's invitations to you, and the Holy Spirit will always be there to support you. Rest assured, Jesus tells us that God can only us to give good things: "What father among you would hand his son a snake when he asks for a fish? ...If you then, who are wicked, know how to give good gifts to your children, how much more will the Father in heaven give the holy Spirit to those who ask him?" (Luke 11:11–13).

BANISH GUILT

We are never completely clean or without fault. Every day we hurt one another; sometimes we don't even realize it. In prayer, these mistakes can make us feel that we are not worthy to receive the gift of God's Holy Spirit. That negative way we think about ourselves prevents the Spirit from acting and transforming us. God does not dwell on our faults, but wants us to share his divine life with us. "Beloved, if [our] hearts do not condemn us, we have confidence in God and receive from him whatever we ask" (John 3:20–21).

REMOVE DOUBT

Maybe you have doubts. Perhaps you think, "God can not do anything for me. I prayed for something, but nothing happened and no one answered. But Jesus says, "Ask and you will receive; seek and you will find; knock and the door will be opened to you. For everyone who asks, receives; and the one who seeks, finds; and to the one who knocks, the door will be opened" (Luke 11:9–10).

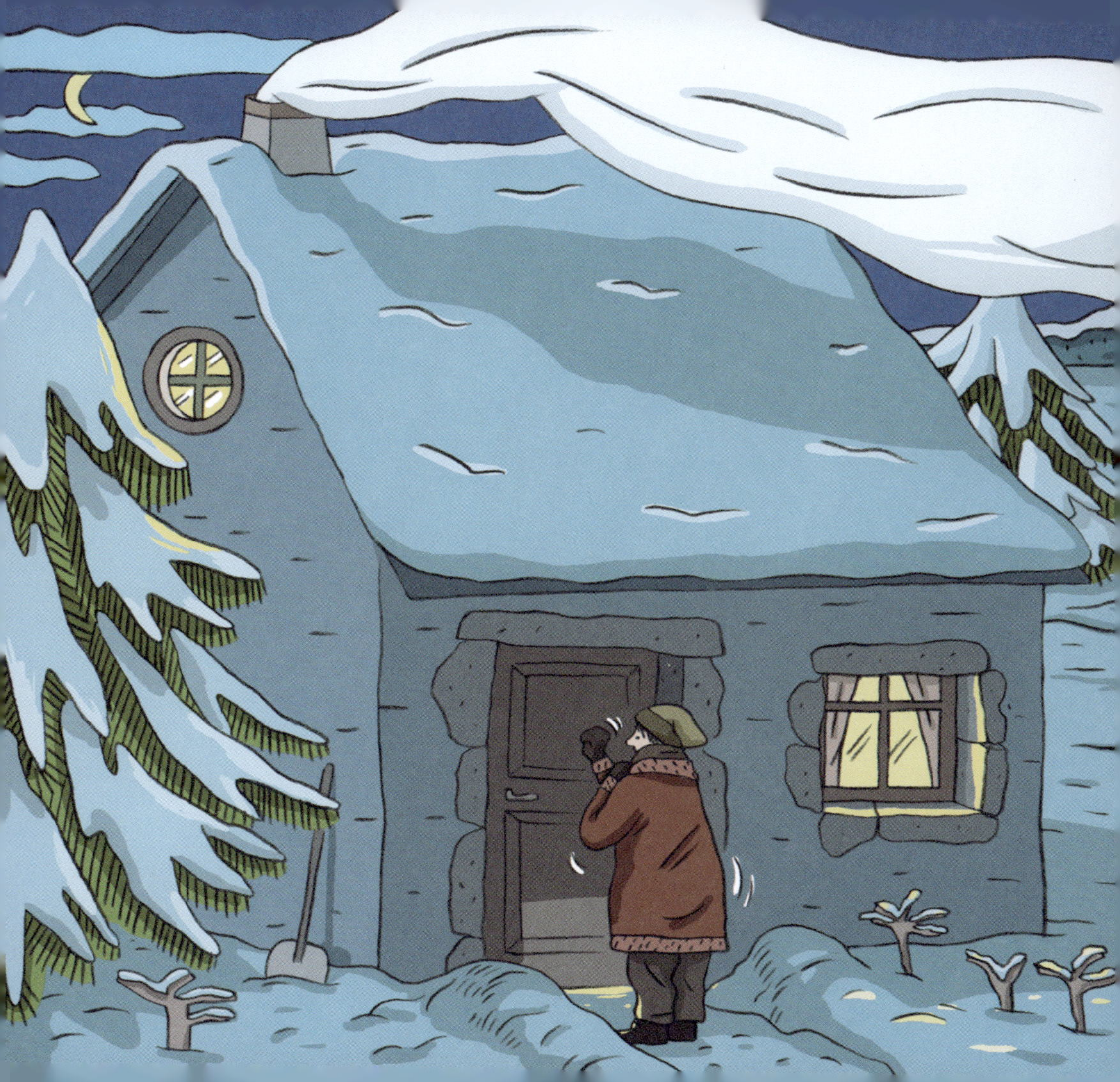

Prayers to the Holy Spirit

Before praying, call on the Holy Spirit. The images of fire, light, and water can help you find the words: "warm, ignite, refresh, quench my thirst." Ask the Spirit to help you to let go of the worries in your life so that you are open to hear what God wants to tell you.

Like a dove

Lord,
I do not know how to pray,
I do not know what to say.
Yet I want to spend a moment
With you.

Send down your Spirit on me
Like a dove.
Put on my lips the words
To speak to you,
To tell you that I love you.

Lord,
Listen to my silence,
You are prayer, you are waiting.
Envelop me with your presence,
Cover me with your Spirit,
Speak, Lord, my heart is ready.

ANNE-SOPHIE DE BOUËTIEZ

Lift me up

Holy Spirit, rushing torrent
Source that purifies everything in its path
Come in our withered hearts
That are without joy

Spirit of Jesus Christ
You who encouraged the Apostles
To go out to announce
Risen Jesus

Come, loosen my tongue
Put words of praise
On my lips

May my voice be beautiful
To sing of my Jesus my Savior
Because I am God's child
It's you who teaches me

Every day
I want to abandon myself to you
Let me carry your breath
Surprising, playful

Seeking the wind
Letting go of the fear that grips me
Lead me to live the adventure
That is prepared for me as God's child!

ANNE-SOPHIE DE BOUËTIEZ

Come, Holy Ghost
(VENI CREATOR)

Come, Holy Ghost, Creator blest,
and in our hearts take up Thy rest;
come with Thy grace and heav'nly aid,
To fill the hearts which Thou hast made.

O Comforter, to Thee we cry,
Thou heav'nly gift of God most high,
Thou Fount of life, and Fire of love,
and sweet anointing from above.

O Finger of the hand divine,
the sevenfold gifts of grace are thine;
true promise of the Father thou,
who dost the tongue with power endow.

Thy light to every sense impart,
and shed thy love in every heart;
thine own unfailing might supply
to strengthen our infirmity.

Drive far away our ghostly foe,
and thine abiding peace bestow;
if thou be our preventing Guide,
no evil can our steps betide.

Praise we the Father and the Son
and Holy Spirit with them One;
and may the Son on us bestow
the gifts that from the Spirit flow.

All glory to the Father be,
With his coequal Son;
The same to thee, great Paraclete,
While endless ages run.

GREGORIAN HYMN OF RABAN MOOR,
BENEDICTINE MONK, NINTH CENTURY

Come, Holy Spirit

Come, Holy Spirit
Holy Spirit, Lord of Light,
From the clear celestial height.
Thy pure beaming radiance give.

Come, thou Father of the poor,
Come, with treasures which endure;
Come, thou Light of all that live!

Thou, of all consolers best,
Thou, the soul's delightful guest,
Dost refreshing peace bestow.

Thou in toil art comfort sweet;
Pleasant coolness in the heat;
Solace in the midst of woe.

Light immortal, Light divine,
Visit thou these hearts of thine,
And our inmost being fill.

If thou take thy grace away,
Nothing pure in man will stay;
All his good is turned to ill.

Heal our wounds, our strength renew;
On our dryness pour thy dew,
Wash the stains of guilt away.

Bend the stubborn heart and will;
Melt the frozen, warm the chill;
Guide the steps that go astray.

Thou, on us who evermore
Thee confess and thee adore,
With thy sevenfold gifts descend.

Give us comfort when we die;
Give us life with thee on high;
Give us joys that never end.
Amen. Alleluia.

SEQUENCE ATTRIBUTED TO STEPHEN LANGDON, ARCHBISHOP OF CANTERBURY

Come, Holy Spirit
(VENI CREATOR)

Come, Holy Spirit,
Come by your wind,
Fill the temple that I am.
Oh, come Holy Spirit, powerful breath,
Breeze of love, stream of life.
Breathe on me, wind of God.

Come, Holy Spirit,
Come by your rain,
Wet the earth that I am.
Oh, come Holy Spirit, impetuous flow,
Source of love, river of life.
Flowing on me, rain of God.

Come, Holy Spirit,
Come by your fire,
Burn the offering that I am.
Oh! Come, Holy Spirit, devouring fire,
Fire of love, flame of life.
Embrace me, fire of God.

ELIZABETH BOURBOUZE,
ALBUM *DEDICATION*, 2005

Spirit of Holiness

Spirit of Holiness,
Come fill our hearts
Deep in our lives,
Awaken your power.

Spirit of Holiness,
Come and fill our hearts
Every day, make us
witnesses of the Lord.

You are the light that comes to enlighten us,
The liberator who comes to deliver us,
The Comforter, Spirit of truth,
In you, hope, and fidelity.

CHRISTIAN SONG, CHEMIN NEUF COMMUNITY

Come, Spirit of Holiness

Come, Spirit of Holiness
Come, Spirit of Light,
Come, Spirit of Fire,
Come and set us ablaze.

Come, Spirit of the Father, be the light,
Bring out from Heaven your splendor
    of glory.

Come, heavenly anointing,
source of living water,
strengthen our hearts and heal
    our bodies.

Spirit of gladness, joy of the Church,
Sprout in our heart the Lamb's song.
Make us recognize the love of the Father,
And reveal to us the Face of Christ.

Fire that illuminates, breath of life,
By you shines the Cross of the Lord.

Truthful witness, you lead us
to proclaim:
Christ is Risen!

ANDRÉ GOUZES,
DOMINICAN MONK AND MUSICIAN

Testimonials

"It was one night in my cell, almost three years ago. Despite all the catastrophes that had fallen on my head for a few months, I remained a convinced atheist.... That night I was in my bed... that is why a cry sprang from my chest, a call for help: 'My God!' Instantly, like a violent wind that seemed to come from nowhere, the Spirit of the Lord took me by the throat.... It was an infinite impression of strength and gentleness that could not be endured too long. And from that moment, I believed, with an unshakable conviction that has not left me since....When the Lord seizes a soul, he does not do it tentatively, but with the brashness of a great Lord."

Jacques Fesch, *Prison Journal, In five hours, I will see Jesus*, ed. Jubilee, 1989.

"I pray often, alone or in a group. I have never received the outpouring of the Spirit, but each time that I invoke the Holy Spirit I feel a lump in my throat and I want to cry. Not sadness, but emotion. I do not know why. What I feel is that it soothes all my tensions and that I enter into a deeper relationship with Christ in prayer."

Isabelle, thirty-one years old

"I never liked all this 'outpouring of the Spirit.' I was always suspicious of it. But one time, I took part in a spiritual retreat. One night, I attended a prayer vigil where one could 'receive the Spirit.' I came because I was friends with the people who were there. I found myself next to the priest who was teaching the retreat. We talked, then he put his hand on my shoulder. When I left, I felt a deep peace and joy."

Renée, eighty-five years old

"My husband was suffering from a serious heart disease. When the doctor told us that he had only one or two months to live, we asked him to receive the Anointing of the Sick. We did not ask for healing, but for the strength to live what we had to live in faith. My husband lived another three-and-a-half years. He did not experience a decline. He was lucid until the end, and he could even attend the wedding of our granddaughter, something he wanted very much."

Huguette, eight-five years old